MAINECOAST
IMPRESSIONS

photography by NANCE TRUEWORTHY

FARCOUNTRY
PRESS
HELENA, MONTANA

Right: It's easy to see why Southwest Harbor, surrounded by Acadia National Park, bills itself as "The Quietside."

Title Page: What could be finer than an afternoon to play on the beach at Reid State Park? The wide, long, sandy beaches were donated to the state by businessman Walter E. Reid in 1946, who stipulated that they be preserved forever.

Cover: An idyllic moment awaits a twosome at Cape Elizabeth. The cape reaches twelve miles into the ocean, creating a sheltered entrance to Casco Bay.

Back cover: Blooming annuals lead your eye to the arching bridge and neatly tended Selectmen's Building, built circa 1780 in Somesville, which now houses a museum operated by the Mount Desert Island Historical Society. Somesville is at the northern end of a seven-mile-long fjord called Somes Sound, on Mount Desert Island.

ISBN 10: 1-56037-438-1
ISBN 13: 978-1-56037-438-1

© 2008 by Farcountry Press
Photography © 2008 by Nance Trueworthy

For more information about our books, write Farcountry Press, P.O. Box 5630, Helena, MT 59604; call (800) 821-3874; or visit www.farcountrypress.com.

Left: Dusk highlights the 1931 Waldo-Hancock Bridge and the new Prospect-Verona Bridge (foreground) spanning the Penobscot River between Prospect and Verona.

Below: Asticou Azalea Garden, in Northeast Harbor near Acadia National Park, includes these serene and simple geometric lines modeled after a Japanese garden.

Right: A picturesque fishing shack sits at the end of Bailey Island, in Casco Bay. Bailey is one of three islands connected by bridges to the mainland near Brunswick.

Far right: A building sports a quaint painted façade, at Camp Ellis, near Saco. Homeowners here must keep a sense of perspective: 1908 records show that the pounding surf has been eroding two to three feet of beach a year. More than thirty homes have been lost to the sea since 1908.

Above: Spring Point Ledge Light looks its finest during the winter holidays. The Portland Harbor Museum adjacent to this functioning lighthouse chronicles the maritime history of the region.

Left: Cuckolds Light sits atop an island just outside Newagen's harbor, near Southport. Its attention-getting moniker may have come from an Englishman who named it for a spit of land in the Thames River reported to have been given by King John to an angry subject, after His Highness had an affair with the man's wife.

Right: Shorebirds depend on Mile Beach, at Reid State Park, for resting and feeding. The area is essential nesting habitat for endangered least terns and piping plovers.

Below: Entwined with this marsh, Rachel Carson National Wildlife Refuge protects discrete segments of coastal salt marshes and estuaries for migratory birds. It was named to honor marine biologist and editor-in-chief for the U.S. Fish and Wildlife Service Rachel Louise Carson (1907–1964). Her book *Silent Spring* is credited with changing the nation's awareness of dangers to the environment.

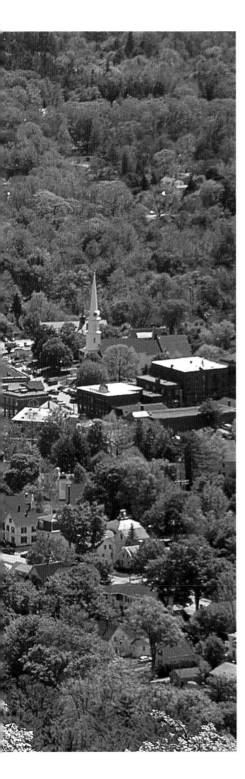

Left: Big, barren ledges of quartzite on top of Mount Battie provide perfect viewing platforms for hikers to see this panorama of Camden and Penobscot Bay. Camden is known for schooner cruises.

Below: Prolific purple loosestrife plants adorn the cliff walk at Prouts Neck, in Scarborough. The artist Winslow Homer lived at Prouts Neck from 1883 until his death in 1910; his paintings made this rocky, rugged coastline famous.

Above: This boat heading for Peaks Island must be sailing over a pot of gold in Casco Bay. The Fifth Maine Regiment Memorial Hall on the island houses a museum that focuses on Civil War and island history.

Right: Maine's 3,500 miles of coastline offer some sandy beaches for surf fishing, such as Pine Point, in Scarborough. Anglers cast for bluefish and striped bass,

Left: Skiffs await their owners at Newagen's harbor, on Southport Island.

Below: The Huntsman Marine Science Centre found 3,317 species living in the Gulf of Maine region in 2006, counted as part of the International Census of Marine Life. Three commonly seen species pictured below are sea stars, sand dollars, and crabs.

Right: The memorial gravestone for Revolutionary War hero Col. Jonathan Buck is in the cemetery at Bucksport. The weathering pattern on the monument is reputed to show the outline of a witch's foot.

Far Right: Historic Fort Knox is across the Penobscot River from Bucksport. Visitors to the fort can access the splendid views of the surrounding river valley from the adjacent 420-foot observation tower.

Below: Construction on the semi-circular Fort Popham was begun in 1862, but never entirely completed. Nevertheless, the granite block structure was used during the Civil War, the Spanish American War, and WWI. It is now a state historic site.

Revere and Sons cast the bell. Subsequently, the bell graced the steeple in the Universalist Church before being moved to the old City Hall in 1861, and moved yet again in 1929 to its current belfry atop City Hall. Every New Year's Eve, Bath residents gather outside City Hall to ring the bell and sing their own lyrics that describe this historical bell, to the tune of "Auld Lang Syne."

Below, left: Tate House, in Portland, preserves period furnishings and the grounds and structure of this pre-Revolutionary home built in 1755 for Captain George Tate. Also in Portland, the Wadsworth-Longfellow House was the childhood home of poet Henry Wadsworth Longfellow. Guided tours provide an overview of the poet's family life.

Below, right: Memorial Chapel is a local landmark on Shore Road in East Boothbay. This nondenominational church built in memory of Janet M. Wilson is very popular for weddings.

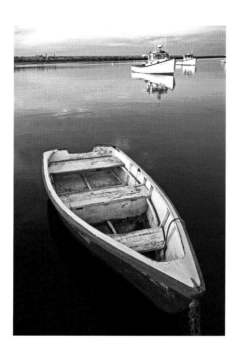

Left: A skiff floats in Camp Ellis's harbor, near Old Orchard Beach. The word skiff is applied to many small, open vessels but generally refers to a light rowboat with a pointed bow and square stern.

Far left: Marshes on Cape Elizabeth provide excellent habitat for waterfowl and wading birds such as this great egret. Overall, Maine has more than 6,000 lakes and ponds, and more than 5,000 rivers and streams. Many are home to land-locked salmon, trout, small-mouth bass, pickerel, and perch.

Below: A duck paddles across a pond at Seawall, on Mount Desert Island.

Above: A pathway beckons visitors to stroll through the emerald greenery in Asticou Azalea Garden, at Northeast Harbor near Acadia National Park. Charles K. Savage built Asticou and the adjacent Thuya gardens in 1956–57.

Left: In 2007 the New England cottontail was listed as endangered in Maine. Often called a "cooney," it is Maine's only native cottontail.

Facing page: A large stone pot anchors one of the delightful groupings in Thuya Gardens, in Northeast Harbor near Acadia National Park. Thuya is the genus of white cedars, which are abundant in this area.

Above: Ogunquit is the Algonquin word meaning "beautiful place by the sea." Ogunquit Beach spans three miles of beautiful sand and sand dunes.

Right: The lobster boat *Jolene Sarah* heads into Cooks Cove, in Casco Bay. The bay holds more than 200 islands, including Orrs Island seen here, which inspired Harriet Beecher Stowe to write *The Pearl of Orr's Island.*

Left: The family-owned, historic Colony Hotel anchors one end of Gooch's Beach, in Kennebunkport. The hotel is one of Maine's first to initiate environmentally responsible practices.

Below: Public art in Portland includes this imaginative painted façade on Free Street.

Right: The focal plane of Bass Harbor Head Light, completed in 1858, stands fifty-six feet above the mean high water mark along Blue Hill Bay on Mount Desert Island. Today's fourth-order Fresnel len repeats a recognizable pattern of three seconds red, one second dark.

Below: Maine's Department of Inland Fisheries and Wildlife estimates the state's moose population at about 29,000. This young bull was seen along the Back Cove Trail, in Portland.

Left: The gardens at Ocean Point, in East Boothbay, provide a colorful backdrop to the scenic vista over the bay.

Below: Flowerbeds of dianthus, nicotiana, echinacea, and lilies grace the grounds of Thuya Gardens in Northeast Harbor, near Acadia National Park.

Right: A raccoon youngster emerges at dusk to forage throughout the night. Raccoons have adapted easily to human activities and thrive throughout most of the state.

Far Right: Granite boulders anchor the coast at Biddeford Pool, a large tidal pool at the mouth of the Saco River.

Below: Gulls fight over alewives, one of ten anadromous fish species native to Maine. Anadromous means the fish swim in from the ocean to spawn in freshwater lakes and ponds.

Left: The square tower holding Hendricks Head Light was erected in 1875 near the Sheepscot River in West Southport. It replaced the original station established in 1829.

Facing page: The twenty-six-foot-tall Portland Breakwater Light (locally called Bug Light) is resplendent at sunset. Fort Gorges is barely discernible in the dim light fading over Casco Bay. Construction on the fort began in 1858 to protect the northeastern approaches to this busy harbor, and it was completed during the Civil War.

Facing Page: Sunset highlights the *Red Lady II* moored among other lobster boats at New Harbor. It is legal to fish for lobsters year-round in Maine, but many fishermen don't head out in mid-winter. It takes up to seven years before a lobster grows large enough to be legally taken; a three-pound lobster is likely fifteen to twenty years old.

Below, left: The unmistakable paint job identifies West Quoddy Head Light. President Thomas Jefferson authorized construction of a lighthouse here. The first tower was completed in 1808 and replaced by this tower and keeper's home in 1858.

Below, right: A festive striped canopy shades passengers riding the Casco Bay Ferry, the primary means of transportation between the islands.

Left: George Washington commissioned this lighthouse, which was first lit in 1791. Named Portland Head Light, on Cape Elizabeth, it is the oldest lighthouse in Maine and the first tower completed by the U.S. government. The nearby keeper's quarters now house The Museum at Portland Head Light, with interpretive displays that showcase lighthouse lenses and history.

Below: Cape Neddick Lighthouse, dubbed Nubble Light, began operating in 1879. The forty-one-foot-high cast-iron tower is lined in bricks; the flashing light can be seen from thirteen nautical miles away.

Right: Boaters drift back to land at Kettle Cove, Cape Elizabeth, at the end of the day.

Far right: South Portland provides a perfect view of the Portland skyline at sunset. Almost a quarter of Maine's population lives in the greater Portland area—230,000 people—and 3.6 million tourists visit Portland annually.

Above: The promise of utter relaxation at Cape Elizabeth beckons visitors. John Smith named this headland in the early 1600s to honor Princess Elizabeth, sister of Charles I of England.

Left: Low tide exposes the salt marsh estuary protected within Wolfe's Neck Woods State Park, near Freeport. The 233-acre park maintains five miles of hiking trails that wind along the shore of Casco Bay and the Harraseeket River, and through the nearby woods.

Facing page: Each summer, Portland's downtown art festival attracts tourists and artists from across the nation. The arts district centered around Congress Street is full of galleries, antiques shops, and art studios in historical buildings, as well as the Portland Museum of Art and other renowned arts institutions.

Below, left: Three inventive steeds await little riders on the carousel at Old Orchard Beach.

Below, right: It's red, white, and blue all over for the Independence Day parade in Ocean Park.

Right: A serene sunset brightens Bass Harbor Marsh, in Acadia National Park.

Far right: Downtown Belfast is known for good restaurants, art galleries, and interesting shops. The Museum in the Streets walking tour has thirty stops that explain the history of Belfast, including the conflagration of 1865 that destroyed 125 downtown buildings.

The Head of the Cape, at Cape Rosier, provides a spectacular view of the islands in Penobscot Bay. People use the harbor for diverse outdoor activities, such as whale watching, kayaking, and fishing. The many islands dotting the harbor are typical of the Maine coastline, which has more than 2,000 islands along its 3,500 miles.

Left: Floats and nets hang on a lobster shack at Cape Neddick. Lobstering and fishing is a way of life on the Maine coast. For instance, in 2004, more than 63 million pounds of lobster were landed, worth more than $253 million.

Below: A worker at the Portland Fish Exchange lumps fish from the hatch of a trawler.

Right and below: Not all of the Maine coast is about whales and lobsters. On shore, you'll see plenty of small land mammals, such as this chipmunk (right) and groundhog (below).

Far right: A quiet moment in the tidal marsh makes the backwaters at Reid State Park a perfect mirror. The nearby dunes rise high enough to protect this salt marsh and the estuarine channels from severe coastal winds.

Left: The shoreline at Bass Harbor provides a nice view of the nearby community of Bernard. Both places are actually part of the Town of Tremont.

Below, left: Lupines adorn a hillside above the bridge at Cozy Harbor, on Southport Island near Boothbay.

Below, right: Wild roses *Rosa rugosa* adorn these rocks on Peaks Island. In the distance, Cushing Island rises in Casco Bay.

Right: Independence Day is celebrated with a big bang throughout the state. Here, fireworks light the night over Portland Harbor.

Below: Edgecomb is built on the granite peninsula created by the Sheepscot and Damariscotta rivers. The area was first settled by EuroAmericans in 1744; the town incorporated in 1774.

Left: This mallard hen has a big brood of ducklings to watch over. Hardy and adaptable, most mallards in Maine are year-round residents.

Far left: Upthrust bedrock reflects the low light of late afternoon near Potts Point, Harpswell Neck.

Below: Combine inventive people with a beach full of white sand, and an intricate sand castle results.

Left and below: An eagle sculpture graces the meditation room at Abbe Museum, in Bar Harbor. The museum focuses on Maine's rich, extensive Native American heritage. The displays include examples from the largest collection of Maine Indian baskets in the Northeast.

Far left: This quiet cove is on Spruce Point, on the Boothbay Harbor peninsula.

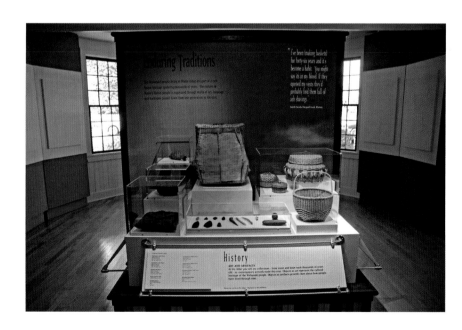

Left: A three-masted windjammer sails into Boothbay Harbor. Sailing aficionados worldwide converge on Boothbay for Windjammer Days, held annually the last week of June.

Below: A mute swan finds refuge in a protected pond. Maine has 2,295 square miles of inland water that support an extensive list of water-dependent birds and other aquatic life. Mute, tundra, trumpeter, and whooper swans inhabit or migrate through Maine.

Right: An established, hardy apple orchard provided the name for Old Orchard Beach. People have been flocking to this sunny strand since the mid-1800s, originally arriving by train from Montreal and Boston.

Below: The stone jetty on Drakes Island serves many purposes, providing a great vantage for fishing as well as wind protection for people simply lounging on the beach.

Left: The waters of Cape Elizabeth's Crescent Beach are drenched in the reflected light of sunset. Cape Elizabeth was established in 1895, when it separated from the greater Portland area.

Below: A tiny table set among the black-eyed Susans invites lingering over the view at Harpswell Neck at dawn.

These pages: A trail along the Stroudwater River winds through nearly three miles of lovely riparian vegetation and scenery in Portland, a "Tree City USA" as designated by the National Arbor Foundation.

Left: Its close proximity to Portland makes Cape Elizabeth's Kettle Cove a popular destination for kayakers.

Below: The dock in Freeport provides a good staging area to sort the day's catch of oysters. Freeport is often described as the birthplace of Maine, because leaders held many debates and made plans to separate from the state of Massachusetts in Freeport's Jameson Tavern. The scheming worked: in 1820, Maine became a state by an Act of Congress.

Left: The full moon creates a dramatic backlight on lobster boats moored in Stonington Harbor, on Deer Isle. It's not always this quiet here. South winds hitting the harbor are known to create very dangerous conditions. Adding to the excitement in summer, Stonington often hosts one of Maine's many lobster boat races.

Below: Wild roses bloom right next to the ocean on Drakes Island, near Wells.

Left: The Castle Tucker in Wiscasset, named for Captain Richard Tucker, preserves this Federal-style mansion built in 1807 on a hill overlooking the Sheepscot River. Inside, visitors see mementos of foreign travel as well as the elaborate furnishings and collected art of a wealthy Victorian family.

Facing page: Brightly colored flowers compete for your attention with the multicolored buoys hanging in a barn in Scarborough.

Right: A rainy day led to this dramatic evening rainbow in Portland Harbor. The kerosene-powered lamp in Spring Point Ledge Light was first lit in 1897; the warning light is now totally automated and powered by electricity.

Below: Cape Rosier is a fine place to view the sun setting over the Camden Hills.

NANCE S. TRUEWORTHY is a photojournalist who specializes in assignment, stock, and location photography. Her work has been published nationally and internationally in books, magazines, calendars, and greeting cards. Nance is the author of five books, *Maine in Four Seasons, Down the Shore, A Seat on the Shore, Maine Impressions,* and *A Guide to the Islands of Casco Bay.* Her photographs appear in the national book series *America 24/7.* Her work was also featured in a Smithsonian Museum exhibit entitled Ocean Planet that traveled throughout the United States. In addition, her photography adorns the exterior of Campus Kerkrade in Rotterdam, The Netherlands, as part of the architecture of the new art center.